Hello, I'm Tatum.

## My background

Name: _____

School: _____

Friends: _____

Interests: _____

_____

_____

_____

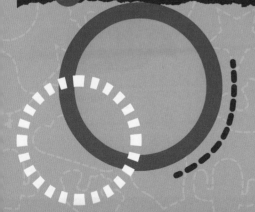

# Before you begin writing ...

Here are the **3Ps** that will help you with your writing: posture, pencil grip and paper position. You will be reminded about these as you go through the book.

## Posture

1. Sit up straight at your table.
2. Put your feet flat on the floor.
3. Keep your wrist straight and resting on the table.

## Pencil or pen grip

1. Rest the pencil or pen on your middle finger.
2. Pinch your index finger and thumb together gently.

Left-handed

Right-handed

## Paper

1. The paper is on an angle and held steady by your non-writing hand.
2. For right-handers, the page will tilt to the left.
3. For left-handers, the page will tilt to the right.

Left-handed

Right-handed

OXFORD UNIVERSITY PRESS

# Revision

**Before you begin, complete the checklist below.**

❏ I have my feet flat on the floor.

❏ My back is up nice and straight.

❏ I can hold the pencil or pen correctly.

print
**a** no exit

cursive
**a** exit

Consolidate your printing of lower-case letters.

a b c d e f g h i j k l m n o p q r s t u v w x y z

Consolidate your printing of capital letters.

A B C D E F G H I J K L M N O P Q R S T U V W X Y Z

Practise these entry and exit flicks.

i j p m n r u v w y l t h k a d m n u i

Consolidate your numerals and punctuation marks.

1 2 3 4 5 6 7 8 9 10 15 20 . , " " ' ? ! ; :

Finish the table below. The first one is done for you.

| 55 489 | Fifty-five thousand, four hundred and eighty-nine |
|---|---|
| 5632 | |
| 15 311 | |
| 5 110 000 | |
| 506 210 | |
| 50 766 | |

Copy the sentences below.

Participating in regular physical activity is good for your health.

It is important to find physical activities that you enjoy.

This can include playing a sport or other types of active

lifestyle habits, such as walking, hiking, gardening or yoga.

## Copy these words

bike riding _____

skateboarding _____

jogging _____

stretching _____

physical _____

gardening _____

# Diagonal joins

Learning intention:
To revise diagonal joins
when forming letters

*in eu*

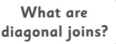

**What are diagonal joins?**

A diagonal join is made from the bottom of one letter to the top of the next letter.

Practise these diagonal joins.

am  an  ap  ar  at  ay  ce  cr  di  dr  dy  he  hu

in  is  le  li  me  mi  ni  nu  te  ti  un  uc  ix  zi

Diagonal joins occur when one letter smoothly transitions to another at an angle. Try not to lift your pencil or pen.

Move along the path without going over the edges.

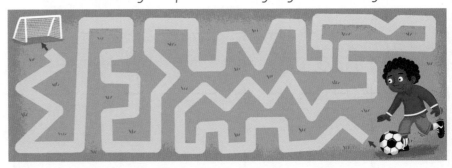

Trace over these letter combinations and then copy them on the lines below. Remember not to lift your pencil or pen.

ni    ni    ni         eu    eu    eu         ne    ne    ne

ep    ep    ep         mi    mi    mi         nu    nu    nu

di    di    di         ip    ip    ip         li    li    li

Use diagonal joins to practise these sentences.

An active lifestyle includes regular physical activity and healthy eating.

This means making an effort to be active throughout the day.

## Word building!

heal

Meaning: to cure or save; make whole, sound and well (from Old English)

Using the base word "heal", how many words can you form?

For example: heal + th = health

Don't forget: we often change the y at the end of a word to an i before adding the suffix.

| Prefix | Base word | Suffixes | | | List your words here |
|--------|-----------|----------|----|----|----------------------|
| un- | heal | -s<br>-ing<br>-ed<br>-er | | | |
| | | -th | -y | -er<br>-est<br>-ly<br>-ness | |

OXFORD UNIVERSITY PRESS

# Diagonal joins to tall letters

Learning intention: To practise our diagonal joins

**I am successful when I can:**
- ❏ sit with my back straight
- ❏ hold the pencil or pen correctly
- ❏ position my paper
- ❏ make diagonal joins smoothly.

## nk ch

A diagonal join is made from the bottom of a lower-case letter to a tall letter.

Use a sweeping movement to practise writing these diagonal joins to tall letters.

al    th    et    ub    d    ch    nk    it    el    ul    lt    lk    at

**Tip!** The crossbar on t needs to be level with the top of the letter body.

activities  _____

fitness  _____

nutrient  _____

active  _____

stretch  _____

Practise these diagonal joins to tall letters.

Playing a sport is a fantastic way of keeping fit and healthy.

There are a variety of sports and activities to engage in.

Enjoying regular physical activity has many health benefits.

## Word building!

Add the suffix -ing to the words below.

Remember to drop the e before adding -ing.
If the last letter is a consonant and comes after a vowel, double the consonant before adding -ing.

swim _____

ride _____

drop _____

bounce _____

skate _____

dance _____

jog _____

hurdle _____

wrestle _____

bike _____

run _____

cycle _____

hop _____

skate _____

**Fine motor skills task:** Help Ava through the maze to find her ball. Be careful not to touch the edges or lift your pencil or pen.

Diagonal joins to tall letters

Practise keeping your letters on the lines. Make sure you keep the size consistent.

good example

# Being active is fun

example of what to avoid

# Being active is fun

Playing a sport isn't the only way to stay fit and healthy. Participating

in a hobby or recreational activity that involves physical movement is

also beneficial for your wellbeing. This could be walking, dancing, hiking,

gardening or taking a yoga class. Select activities that you enjoy and

that get you moving, and then do them regularly.

**Self-assessment** Draw a star next to your best writing. Think about size, slope and how well you completed your diagonal joins.

Practise your keyboarding skills by typing the above passage.

Diagonal joins to tall letters

# Drop-in joins

**What are drop-in joins?**

When we do a diagonal join to an anti-clockwise letter, the exit from the first letter reaches high towards the top of the next letter. We then drop the next letter in place.

Drop-in joins help to make smooth transitions from the ending stroke of one letter to the starting stroke of the next letter. This avoids retracing and contributes to the legibility and elegance of cursive handwriting.

slide left

Extend exit, lift and drop in the next letter.

ā  ia

The letters a, c, d, g, o and q are dropped into place.

ac  ca  dg  eq  ma  da  oa  ac  ca  dg  ma  oa  ac

Write these drop-in joins. The dot shows you when to lift the pencil or pen.

na  ma  ic  ud  aq  ug  id  eg  ec  nd  iq  da  ig  ed  uc  ag

Practise these drop-in joins.

fantastic  sweat  exercise  start  agility  light  edge

sport  posture  balance  powerful  conditioning  stretch

muscles  body  workout  training  practise  athletic

**Self-assessment**  Underline your smoothest join. Circle a join that needs more practice.

Copy the sentences below, practising your drop-ins and holding your pencil or pen correctly.

Active games and family activities are other fun ways to lead an

active lifestyle. Games such as hide and seek, capture the flag, tip and

hopscotch are all fun and engaging activities. Enjoying the outdoors is a

great way of being physically active. Try bike riding, going for a bush

walk or playing a game in the park. The whole family can enjoy being

active together. Make it fun and do it often to feel the benefits.

**Fine motor skills task:** Follow the steps to draw the picture.

# Horizontal joins

small dip

retrace

retrace

## or rā ok

Learning intention:
To use horizontal joins for
o, r, v, w and x

Horizontal joins are made from letters that finish near the top.

Practise these horizontal joins.

oi   om   on   op   or   ot   ou   ov   ow   ox   rb   ri   rm   rn

ru   rv   rw   va   vi   vo   wi   wa   wn   wo   xi   xp

outings   boost   workout   development   explore   exciting   crucial

## Word building!

Build three or more words from the base words, choosing the right suffixes from below. The first one is done for you.
−ment, −ed, −ing, −able, −y, −ive, −ion

Don't forget: we usually drop the e at the end of words when adding a suffix.

| excite | excitement | excited | exciting |
|---|---|---|---|
| discover | | | |
| participate | | | |
| engage | | | |
| interact | | | |
| cooperate | | | |
| coordinate | | | |
| enjoy | | | |

# Horizontal joins from f

**I am successful when I can:**
- ❏ sit with my back straight
- ❏ hold the pencil or pen correctly
- ❏ position my paper
- ❏ make my joins to f straight.

When joining horizontally to f, the join is straight.

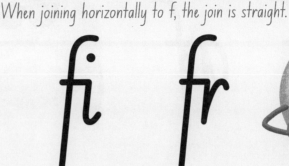

*fr* *fu* *fi* *fr* *fu* *from* *funny* *friendship* *finishing* *fitness*

The letter f doesn't join to e. When f joins to l, retrace the downstroke on the l.

*fl* *fe* *fl* *fe* *flapping* *flexibility* *fearless*

Remember to retrace when joining f to a and o.

*fa* *fo* *fa* *fo* *family* *footwear* *follow*

**Fine motor skills task:** Draw a picture of you and your family or friends having fun.

*Family fun with games and sports is a wonderful way to promote*

*physical activity among family members. Some ideas for family-friendly*

*games and sports include playing hide and seek, swimming and hiking.*

**Self-assessment**   Draw a star next to your best writing. Think about size, slope and how well you completed your diagonal joins.

# Joins to f

uf af

Remember, to make a diagonal join to f, lift your pencil or pen and drop the f onto the exit flick of the letter in front.

Remember to lift your pencil or pen when joining to f. Practise by tracing the letters and then copying them.

ef    ef _____

uf    uf _____

af    af _____

if    if _____

surfing    often    brief    mischief    careful    roof    leaf    softball

Copy the picture of the surfer in the box provided.

# Joins to s

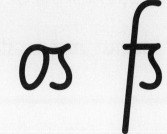

**I am successful when I can:**

☐ sit with my back straight
☐ hold the pencil or pen correctly
☐ position my paper
☐ make my joins to s go across the top and then retrace.

When joining diagonally or horizontally to s, create a short flick at the top of the s and then retrace on the way down.

Practise these joins to s.

os    rs    fs    ws    us    is    as    ts    ls    ns    us    es

lost    toss    history    activities    emphasis    composes    occurs

On the lines below, practise joining the s with a diagonal join, making the top of the s shorter.

Australian sport has a rich and diverse history, with a strong emphasis on

outdoor activities and both traditional and modern sports. Among the most

popular sports are tennis, cricket, netball, soccer and Australian rules football.

Copy these words with joins to s onto the lines below. Underline the words that use a horizontal join to s.

news    best    muscle    stress    socks    household    stamina    most

speed skating    members    drawstring    positive    sustain    offside

Copy these words with joins to s onto the lines below. Underline the words that use diagonal joins to s.

skates  tennis  rackets  students  skills  matches  games  blossom  memories  fastest

Which letters always come before
a horizontal join to s?

Rewrite these words, adding all possible joins.

because    _____

most    _____

emphasis    _____

activities    _____

**Fine motor skills task:** Practise your drawing skills by following these examples to build a picture.

# Joins to double s

**I am successful when I can:**
- ❏ sit with my back straight
- ❏ hold the pencil or pen correctly
- ❏ position my paper
- ❏ make my double s clear.

horizontal join to s

## gloss  glass

diagonal join to s

Copy the words below to practise writing double s.

pass  bossy  motocross  passing  toss  success  lacrosse  miss

tossing  crossbar  dismissal  loss  wilderness  stress  breathless

In the game of cricket, a dismissal is when a batter goes out. There are

a few ways a batter can be dismissed. Common forms of dismissal

include being caught, bowled or run out. The outcome of the game may

hinge on the toss of the coin, because conditions that one side faces

now compared to conditions the other side faces later on can dictate

the success or struggles for each team throughout the match.

# Joins to o, r, k

small dip

retrace

retrace

retrace

*or ra ok*

Horizontal joins are made from letters that finish near the top.

Practise these horizontal joins.

or   ra   oy   re   oo   rt   wi   od   ot   or   on   os   vi

ri   wn   rr   ro   om   ot   wd   og   ov   vi   rt   we   ow

There are many other sports that Australians enjoy, such as

basketball, swimming, golf, surfing, cycling and more. Sport plays

an important role in Australian culture, by providing entertainment

and promoting physical fitness and community engagement.

In cursive handwriting, complete each sentence below, adding the correct punctuation mark at the end of each sentence.

My favourite sport is _____ because _____

Sport is great because _____

At school we play _____

OXFORD UNIVERSITY PRESS

# Joins to e

**I am successful when I can:**
- ☐ sit with my back straight
- ☐ hold the pencil or pen correctly
- ☐ position my paper
- ☐ make my joins to e connect horizontally, creating a smooth line.

bigger dip

*oe  re*

When joining horizontally to e, some letters have a bigger dip than a normal horizontal join. This makes it easier to join.

Practise these horizontal joins to e.

re    ve    we    oe    xe    re    ve    we    oe    xe

are    have    give    fervent    persevere    unwavering    relaxed

Participating in sport can have a powerful impact on children, as it can

give them the chance to develop physical capabilities and teamwork skills,

and learn the value of dedication and hard work. Children who are

fervent and passionate about their sport persevere through challenges,

have unwavering commitment and strive for excellence.

| Word | Part of speech | Meaning | Image |
|------|---------------|---------|-------|
| persevere | verb | To keep trying and not give up, even though it is difficult. | |
| fervent | adjective | To have strong feelings about something and be very sincere and enthusiastic about it. | |
| strive | verb | To make a great effort to do or achieve something. | |

Answer these questions using cursive handwriting.

How do you stay on track when trying to persevere with a difficult task?

What is something you are fervent about?

What are you striving to achieve?

**Self-assessment**

Think about your work in relation to the success criteria.
What did you notice you were able to do well?
What do you need to work on next?

# Letters that do not join

As with capital letters, we do not add joins to letters that finish in a clockwise direction. So you can see that b, g, j, p, s and y do not join. (When we add speed loops, they can join, but not yet.) Can you find them on this page?

Practise your cursive handwriting by copying these commonly misspelt words.

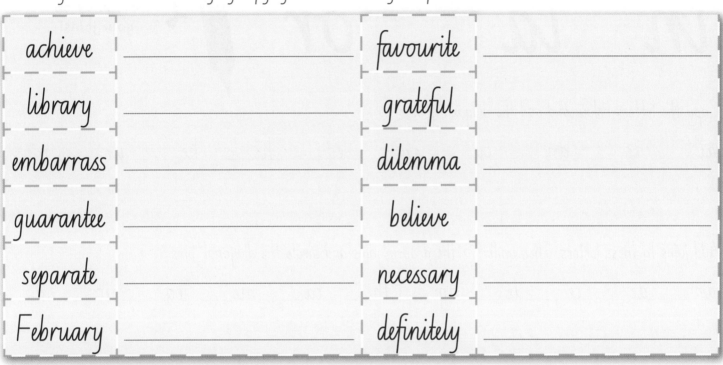

| | | | |
|---|---|---|---|
| achieve | _____ | favourite | _____ |
| library | _____ | grateful | _____ |
| embarrass | _____ | dilemma | _____ |
| guarantee | _____ | believe | _____ |
| separate | _____ | necessary | _____ |
| February | _____ | definitely | _____ |

Copy the text below, remembering that some letters do not join because they finish in a clockwise direction.

Playing a sport promotes opportunities to form new friendships and

learn new skills. It also brings joy and develops a sense of

belonging, boosting self-esteem and improving overall health. Apart

from the benefits to physical health, playing a sport also helps

to build confidence, resilience, pride and a positive attitude.

# Consolidating

Diagonal         Drop-in         Horizontal

Extend exit, lift and
drop-in the next letter.

small dip

*in*        *ia*        *or*

**Brush up on your joins!**

Copy the letters below and add the diagonal joins.

ai    as    an    cu    in    es    hi    ke    ur    me

Add joins to these letters. Then underline the drop-in joins and circle the diagonal joins.

ar    de    ce    le    ag    th    ca    me    ea    ua    do

Write this sentence adding in joins, including drop-in joins.

Engaging in sport provides quality opportunities for recreation and leisure.

Add the joins.

It also provides a source of leisure and a break from daily routines.

Copy this sentence to practise joining to the letter s.

It is essential to participate in sport with the correct safety equipment.

# Assessment: Joins

Rewrite these words in cursive, adding in joins.

| | | | |
|---|---|---|---|
| fitness | _____ | boost | _____ |
| because | _____ | often | _____ |
| benefits | _____ | promote | _____ |
| careful | _____ | balance | _____ |
| members | _____ | active | _____ |
| workout | _____ | health | _____ |
| explore | _____ | physical | _____ |
| theme | _____ | found | _____ |
| tennis | _____ | soccer | _____ |

Copy the passage below to practise your joins.

Sports offer numerous benefits, such as improved fitness and family fun.

Many different types of leisure activities, including walking, hiking and

playing games, also help to promote wellbeing and healthy lifestyle habits.

Teacher feedback

 Practise your keyboarding skills by typing this passage.

# Fluency joins

## Fluency joins from b, p, s

**What are fluency joins?**

*be pl su*

Retrace the bottom of the letter.

Fluency joins help us to write faster and be more consistent with size and slope. We now add base joins to these letters: b, p and s.

Copy the fluency joins from the letters b, p and s in all the letter pairs and words below.

ba    bb    be    bi    bl    bo    br    bu    by    pa    pe    pi

pl    pp    po    pr    pu    py    sa    se    si    sl    so    sp    ss    su

busy        keep        several        select        pride

Make sure you retrace the bottom of the letter before you join to the next letter.

basketball        softball        bowling        pentathlon

powerlifting        sailing        pilates        baseball

When joining to a tall letter, go right to top of the letter, then retrace as you come back down.

applause        hobby        ribbon        physical

platform diving        show jumping        blading

# Practising fluency joins

Practise your fluency joins by adding joins from the
letters b, p and s on this page and the next.

## Badminton

Badminton is a racket sport played by two or more

players. Players use lightweight rackets to strike a

shuttlecock. Badminton is played at various skill

levels, from backyard games to highly competitive international tournaments.

## Softball

Softball is a team sport usually played on a field.

It requires a combination of skills, such as batting,

throwing, catching and base running. Softball

provides great opportunities to develop skills, learn

about teamwork and engage in friendly competition.

## Netball

Netball is a popular sport incorporating skills such as passing and shooting. Players must work together to pass and catch the ball while trying to outmanoeuvre the other team. The game is played in schools, leagues and at the international level.

## Soccer

Soccer is one of Australia's most popular sports. It has a long and rich history in many countries around the world and is sometimes referred to as the "world game". It is a fast-paced game, with players requiring skilful footwork, agility and endurance.

# Fluency joins with double s

To increase the speed of our writing, for words that use ss, we will now make the second s the same style as the first s. This means we can keep our pen on the page instead of lifting it to write the second s.

Copy these cursive letter pairs.

oss        ess        iss        uss        oss        ess        iss        uss

Practise using cursive handwriting by copying these commonly confused words and their definitions.

lesson – a fixed time when people are taught about a subject or how to do something

lessen – to become or make something become smaller, weaker or less important

**Fine motor skills task:** Follow the steps and complete the drawing.

# Consolidating

Copy this passage.

Australian rules football is a fast-paced and physical game involving

players advancing the ball by either kicking it or handpassing it.

The objective of the game is to score the highest points. Each goal is

worth six points, and each behind is worth one point. A behind is

when the ball goes through the behind posts, which are placed on either

side of the goal posts. Before Australian rules football, there was the

First Nations sport known as marngrook. This game involved kicking

and catching a ball made from possum or kangaroo skin.

Teacher feedback

Practise your keyboarding skills by typing this passage.

OXFORD UNIVERSITY PRESS

# Assessment: Fluency joins

Copy these words to practise your fluency joins.

spectators    brave    premier    strong    showcase    pitch

bases    penalty    strike    pass    sailing    blindside

Copy this passage to practise your fluency joins.

People love to not only participate in sport but also to be spectators.

Spectators love watching and cheering on their favourite teams and

sportspeople in a variety of sports, including swimming, sailing, motocross,

tennis, volleyball and football. Watching sports with other spectators is

exciting and fun. Perhaps more importantly, it can also provide a sense

of belonging and camaraderie.

 **Self-assessment** Draw a star next to your best writing. Think about size, slope and how well you completed your fluency joins.

# Speed loops

## Speed loops to and from f

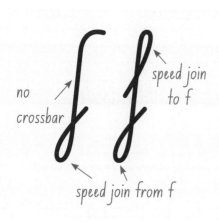

no crossbar

speed join to f

speed join from f

What are speed loops?

Speed loops are fluid movements used to create loops and curves in the letters of a word. Speed loops should cross at the baseline.

speed loop from f

Practise writing the letter f at the beginning of a word.

fa    fa    fr    fr    fe    fe    fi    fi    fl    fl    fo    fo

field        fairness        fantastic        futsal        frisbee

speed loop to f

speed loop from f

Practise writing f to and from other letters.

oft    oft    aft    aft    ife    ife    ifu    ifu    afy    afy

leafy    beautiful    life    after    before    referee    often

speed loop at the end of a word

crossbar

Practise writing when f is the last letter of a word.

ef    ef    urf    urf    iff    iff    uff    uff    rf    rf    af    af

surf    bluff    puff    self    proof    chief    turf

OXFORD UNIVERSITY PRESS

# Speed loops from g, j and y

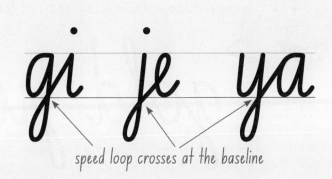

speed loop crosses at the baseline

Practise these speed loops from g.

ga    ge    gi    gl    go    gr    gu    ga    ge    gi    gl    go    gr

golf    gymnastics    goalkeeper    game    grip    goalie    grade

Practise these speed loops to and from j.

ja ju ji jo ja ju jumping juggling joggers join just adjust subject

Practise these speed loops to and from y.

ya    ye    yi    yo    yu    yl    yr    ya    ye    yi    yo    yu    yl    yr

yachting    yoga    yellow    young    yearly    yaw    yard

Speed loops from body and tail letters should cross at the baseline.

*gold jump yacht*

speed loop crosses at the baseline

Practise your speed loops by copying these words, which are commonly misspelt.

| jewellery | | judgement | |
|-----------|--|-----------|--|
| challenge | | congratulate | |
| rhythm | | hygiene | |

Practise your speed loops by copying these sentences.

The sport of gymnastics is challenging, with athletes needing a

combination of strength, agility, flexibility and coordination.

Gymnastics dates back thousands of years, with roots in Ancient Greece,

where it formed part of the physical training for soldiers.

**I am successful when I can:**

- ☐ sit with my back straight
- ☐ hold the pencil or pen correctly
- ☐ position my paper
- ☐ use speed loops to increase my fluency and speed.

*jersey*

no loop

Remember that body and tail letters don't have a speed loop when the letter comes at the end of the word.

Practise your speed loops by copying this passage.

The "yellow jersey" is a term used in cycling, particularly in one of the most

famous races: the Tour de France. The Tour de France is typically held annually

in July. It consists of multiple stages, which can include flat stages, mountain

stages, time trials and more. The rider who wears the yellow jersey at the end of

each stage is recognised as the race leader. Wearing the yellow jersey is a significant

honour in the sport of cycling and often indicates that the rider is a strong

contender for winning the overall race.

Practise your keyboarding skills by typing this passage.

**Self-assessment**  Draw a star next to your best writing. Think about size, slope and how well you completed your speed loops.

# Speed loops to b, h, k and l

speed loop crosses at the top body line

**Learning intention:**
To use speed loops to increase fluency and speed when writing

**I am successful when I can:**
☐ use speed loops from body and tail letters
☐ cross speed loops across the top body line.

**Tip!** The letters b, k, h and l do not need a speed loop when they appear at the start of a word.

Practise these speed loops to b, h, k and l on this page and the next.

b    b    b    b    ab    be    ib    ob    ub    bb    lb    rb    bl

able    table    football    volleyball    tribe    able    bulb    robe

h    h    h    h    oh    gh    ph    sh    th    ch    ah    oh    gh

triathlon    shine    think    thigh    marathon    workout    archery

To enhance their agility and strength, football players often work out at the gym.

Becoming a football player requires skill, hard work and confidence.

Try not to make your speed loops too big or they will slow down your writing.

al   cl   dl   el   il   gl   ll   lm   ln   ol   pl   rl   sl   tl

golf   cycling   wrestling   athletics   goalie   walk   happily   volley

k   k   k   k   ak   ek   ck   ok   lk   nk   rk   sk   uk

walk   risk   work   rink   kick   jacket   kayak   strike   kit

Copy this sentence, focusing on your speed loops.

Soccer, also known as football in many parts of the world, involves

a wide range of skills that players need to learn in order to excel.

Players need to kick the ball towards the goal and to move swiftly

across the field by passing, dribbling and controlling the ball.

**Peer feedback**

Ask a partner to review your work and provide feedback on how well you completed your speed loops.

Two stars (two things you did well)

⭐ _____

⭐ _____

One wish (one suggestion on something you can improve)

_____

**I am successful when I can:**
- ❑ sit with my back straight
- ❑ hold the pencil or pen correctly
- ❑ position my paper
- ❑ cross speed loops at the body line.

loops cross at the body line

*ph  ck*

 Remember, speed loops to ascenders cross at the body line.

Copy these words with speed loops that cross at the body line.

martial        wrestling        bowling        racquetball        kiteboarding

mountaineering        snowboarding        badminton        hurdles        archery

Remember, the loop is only used when joining to these letters, not if the word ends with these letters.

✓ jumping        NOT        jumping ✗

no loop

Practise your speed loops by copying these words.

| | | | |
|---|---|---|---|
| bowling | _____ | strike | _____ |
| hockey | _____ | pucks | _____ |
| physical | _____ | walking | _____ |
| kayaking | _____ | paddling | _____ |

Remember not to make your speed loops too big or they will slow you down.

Practise your speed loops by copying the passage below.

The word "football" can have different meanings depending on the region you live in.

It is a term used to describe a variety of different types of sports involved in kicking

a ball to score goals. Around the world, the word "football" is associated with what

Australians call soccer. In the United States of America, "football" means a different

type of sport, called gridiron. The field is divided into sections by yard lines, and the

game is played with a combination of passing, running and kicking, with the

primary focus being to get the ball into the opponent's end zone to score points.

# Speed loops to and from z

Speed loops make joining letters faster and quicker. They help with fluency because there is less retracing of letters. Adding a new descender to z helps to join these letters faster.

✗ OLD       ✓ NEW

z ⟶ z

Practise these speed loops with the new z.

z    z    z    zoo    zap    zip    buzz    fuzzy    jazz    fizz

Copy this passage with cursive handwriting and speed loops.

Australia has a rich history of producing sporting champions who have

achieved amazing success. A few notable Australian sporting heroes include

Sir Donald Bradman, Dawn Fraser, Rod Laver, Raelene Boyle, Evonne

Goolagong Cawley, Shane Gould, Shane Warne, Cathy Freeman, Ian

Thorpe and Dylan Alcott. These are just a few examples of Australian

sporting heroes who have made a significant contribution to their sport.

**Self-assessment**    Draw a star next to your best writing. Think about size, slope and how well you completed your speed loops.

    Practise your keyboarding skills by typing this passage.

# Building fluency with speed loops

## Apple and bran muffins

Practise your speed loops by copying these ingredients.

### Ingredients

2 cups self-raising flour, sifted

$\frac{1}{2}$ teaspoon baking powder, sifted

1 cup wheat bran

2 tablespoons brown sugar

1 teaspoon ground cinnamon

1 large pink lady apple, grated

1 cup skim milk

2 eggs, lightly beaten

2 tablespoons vegetable oil

$\frac{1}{2}$ cup apple sauce

Practise your keyboarding skills by typing this recipe procedure.

Place flour, baking powder, bran, sugar, cinnamon and apple in a large bowl. Stir to combine. Make a well in the centre. Place milk, eggs, oil and apple sauce into a jug and whisk until just combined. Pour mixture into well and stir gently. Scoop the batter into the muffin tin. Bake for 15 minutes at 170 degrees Celsius. You will be able to smell when they are cooked.

# Consolidating

Copy these sentences to practise your speed loops and fluency joins.

Dylan Alcott is an Australian wheelchair tennis player

and disability advocate. He is known for his remarkable achievements in wheelchair

tennis and his efforts to promote inclusivity and equality for people with disabilities.

Cathy Freeman is a track and field athlete who is celebrated as one of

Australia's greatest sporting heroes. She is an Olympic gold medallist who

lit the Olympic flame in Sydney. Freeman's athletic skill and unwavering

determination have earned her a special place in Australian hearts.

Shane Warne was inducted into the Sport Australia Hall of Fame

in 2009 for his contribution to cricket. He transformed the art of

leg spin, a type of spin bowling in cricket. Warne's impact on cricket

was immense and he remains a cricketing legend in Australia.

OXFORD UNIVERSITY PRESS

# Assessment: Speed loops

Rewrite the words below, adding speed loops to the letters that need them.

triumph     legend     challenge     achievement     recognition     symbol

celebrate     skilful     jogging     potential     excellence     heritage

Practise your cursive handwriting with speed loops by copying this information about Sir Donald Bradman.

Sir Donald Bradman was inducted into the Sport

Australia Hall of Fame in 1985. On that occasion,

he said that if anyone deserves a statue, they should be

someone who has lived their life with dignity, integrity,

courage and modesty. These qualities are in addition to their skill, and are

compatible with pride, ambition and competitiveness.

Teacher feedback

 Practise your keyboarding skills by typing this passage.

## Spacing

It is important to keep your spacing even between letters and words. This will help to make your writing more legible.

# sporting champions

Copy the text below, focusing on the fluency joins and speed loops. Remember that tall letters, capitals and numerals are the same height.

Some types of motorsports include the 1000 km touring car race

Bathurst 1000 and the Australian Grand Prix, an annual motor racing

event. Drivers have to be very fit to cope with the force on the car and

their bodies as they drive at such fast speeds. These sporting events provide

exciting and thrilling experiences for both participants and spectators.

**Fine motor skills task:** Copy the drawing.

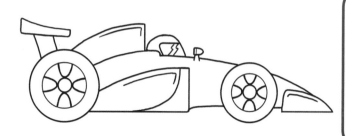

OXFORD UNIVERSITY PRESS

# Size

**I am successful when I can:**
- ❏ sit with my back straight
- ❏ hold the pencil or pen correctly
- ❏ position my paper
- ❏ make my letters even in size and keep them between the lines.

Focus on keeping your letter size between the lines, as it helps to make your writing easier to read.

Practise your cursive handwriting.

Tennis is not only a competitive sport

but also a popular recreational activity

and a fun way to stay physically active.

The Australian Open is a Grand Slam tournament held annually in

Melbourne. Wheelchair tennis follows the same rules as traditional tennis

but with a few changes to assist players using wheelchairs. It promotes

inclusivity, giving individuals with mobility impairments an opportunity

to participate in an active and competitive sport.

# Slope

Use the slope grids below (or the slope card at the back of the book) to help you maintain a consistent slope.

recreation

improvement

technique

perseverance

strength

flexibility

## Fine motor skills task:

Using these images, create a drawing that reminds you of being active, relaxing or doing something you really enjoy in the outdoors.

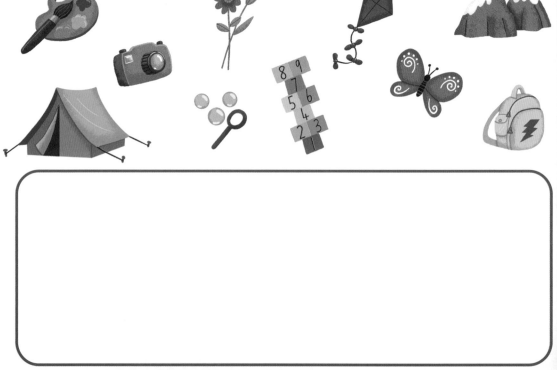

# Developing your signature

Below are some examples of signature styles.

*Signature Signature Signature*

**Tip!** Everyone needs to put their signature on various documents. Signatures are used when you are signing important documents, such as work forms, letters and certificates. It is important that your signature be unique and easy to write.

Practise your signature below. Try out a few different versions.

_____     _____

_____     _____

_____     _____

Select your favourite version and keep practising it below, so that it becomes automatic.

_____     _____

_____     _____

_____     _____

# Punctuation

Commas are punctuation marks used in writing to separate items in a list or indicate a pause in a sentence.

Copy the sentences below to practise using commas.

## Beach volleyball

Beach volleyball is one of the most popular recreational activities in the world.

It became an Olympic sport at the 1996 games, held in Atlanta, Georgia, in the USA.

## Skiing

Skiing is popular in places with snowy climates

such as Norway, Canada, Switzerland and Italy.

There are many types of skiing, including downhill, alpine and cross-country skiing.

## Table tennis

Table tennis, which is similar to ping-pong, is

popular in many Asian countries, including

China, Vietnam and the Philippines. It is played indoors and is a fast-paced game.

# Consolidating

Copy the words in the spaces below and consolidate maintaining consistent slope.

batsman          wickets          pitch          innings

|||||||||||||||||||||    |||||||||||||||||||    |||||||||||||||||||    |||||||||||||||||||||

fielding          stumps          international          boundary

|||||||||||||||||||||    |||||||||||||||||||    |||||||||||||||||||    |||||||||||||||||||||

Rewrite the following words with the appropriate spacing between the letters.

bowlers          run out          delivery          dismissal          tournament

Copy the sentences below, and then check the size of your letters.

Cricket is one of Australia's favourite outdoor sports, with matches lasting from

a few hours to several days. It is a sport that requires endurance, skill and strategy.

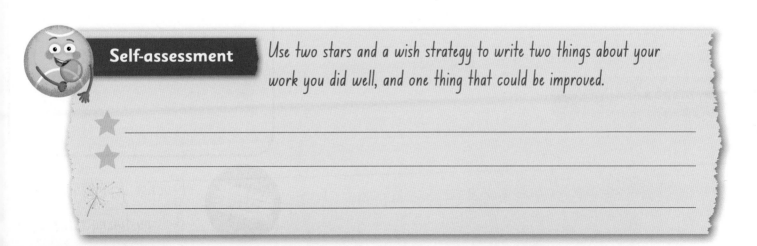

**Self-assessment**  Use two stars and a wish strategy to write two things about your work you did well, and one thing that could be improved.

⭐ _____

⭐ _____

✳ _____

# Assessment: Fluency and legibility

Copy the text below, focusing on your size, spacing and slope.

Softball is a team sport that involves two opposing teams hitting a pitched ball

and running around a series of bases to reach home plate. A run is scored when

a baserunner safely touches all three bases and reaches home plate. Each team

has nine players, each of whom gets a turn to bat and to field. Softball is a sport

played by all ages and skill levels throughout

Australia. Softball is similar to baseball, but

the field is smaller, the ball is bigger and only

underhand pitches are allowed.

**Fine motor skills task:** Select two of your favourite pictures and sketch them in the box below.

**Teacher feedback**

 Practise your keyboarding skills by typing this passage.